Have you ever met someone and they became your best friend? That happened with my au pair. I want to share with you how awesome having an au pair is.

An au pair is someone who comes from another country to help take care of my brothers, sisters and me. Before she came to live with us, we got to meet her on the computer.

That was so cool. Her accent was different but she seemed so fun and was excited to come to America.

I do think our au pair was sad to leave her family even if she was excited to come be with us.

It was so exciting to make signs, pick flowers and drive to pick her up from the airport. She had flown all the way across the ocean just to be with us. That shows me how special our family is. And how special she is.

After the airport, we took her out to dinner then showed her where she would be living with us. We set up her room special with new pillows, furniture and flowers.

During her time with us, we had a lot of fun. One of my favorites was her trying American food and drinks. The faces she made when trying rootbeer were so funny. We all laughed and laughed, as she laughed too.

Having an au pair is a great way to learn about other countries. Our au pair often cooked her favorite foods that her mommy used to cook for her.

We also got to take her on a trip for her very first rollercoaster ride. Her first was one was one of the biggest in America. That was pretty special to share that with her!

While hanging around the house we loved dressing up and taking fun selfies. When she leaves we are going to love having these pictures to look at. We also send these pictures to her family so they can see how happy she is!

We also love holidays, especially Halloween. Our Au Pair's country doesn't celebrate Halloween the way we do in America. She carved her very first pumpkin and helped us carve ours. We then got dressed up and went out Trick or Treating for candy. This was a very special moment.

While she was here, we went to all these awesome places so she could see how different America can be from state to state. We took her to Texas and she was surprised at how big the Longhorns are and loved the food. We love Texas too, so it was fun to share this experience with her.

As my mom often says "All good things must come to an end." Our au pair's time in America went by really fast but it was full of hugs and love. She took care of us while we were sick, when our parents had to work, and became a member of our family. We loved having her here and were sad she had to go home, but that is what au pairs have to do. They miss their families also.

The best part of her time with us are the memories and pictures. We love her, she loves us and know that we will never forget each other. Because we are family.

Rachel Brenke is an author and lawyer for small business owners. She currently lives in Northern Virginia with her husband, five kids and dog Archer.

For more books visit www.rachelbrenke.com

Made in the USA
Middletown, DE
01 September 2016